easy solos for beginning cello

level 1

by craig duncan

Online PDF www.melbay.com/94659EB

Contents

	Cello	Piano
Russian Dance Tune	4	4
Ode to Joy (Beethoven)	5	5
Kum Bah Yah	6	6
Country Gardens	7	7
Yankee Doodle	8	8
Largo from *The New World Symphony* (Dvorak)	9	9
Fanfare Minuet (Duncombe)	10	10
King William's March (Clarke)	11	11
Dixie (Emmett)	12	12
Gavotte (Telemann)	13	14
Soldier's March (Schumann)	14	15
German Dance (Beethoven)	15	16
Symphony Theme (Brahms)	16	17
Dona Nobis Pacem	17	18
Ash Grove	18	19

Russian Dance Tune

Folk Song

Ode to Joy

Ludwig van Beethoven

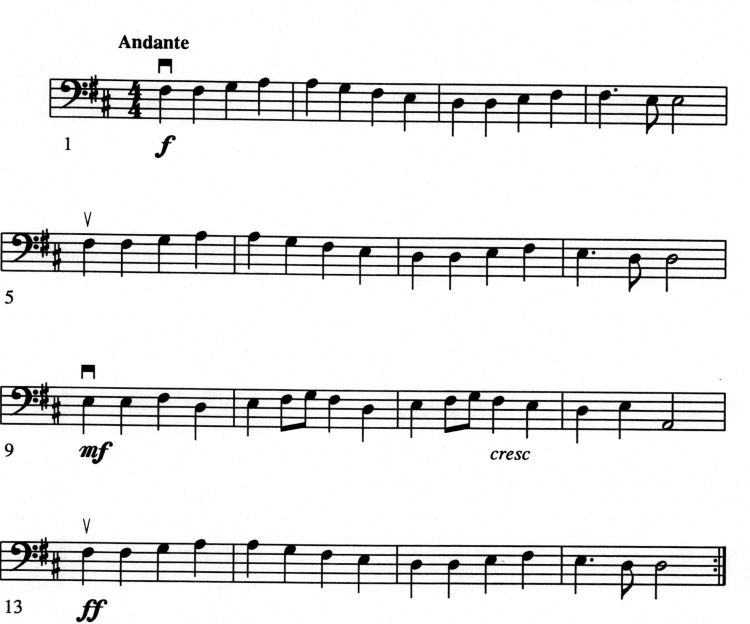

Kum Bah Yah

African Folk Melody

Country Gardens

English Dance Tune

Yankee Doodle

American Folk Tune

Largo

from The New World Symphony

Anton Dvorak

Fanfare Minuet

William Duncombe

King William's March

Jeremiah Clarke

Dixie

D. D. Emmett

Gavotte

Georg Philipp Telemann

Soldier's March
from Album for the Young

Robert Schumann

German Dance

Ludwig van Beethoven

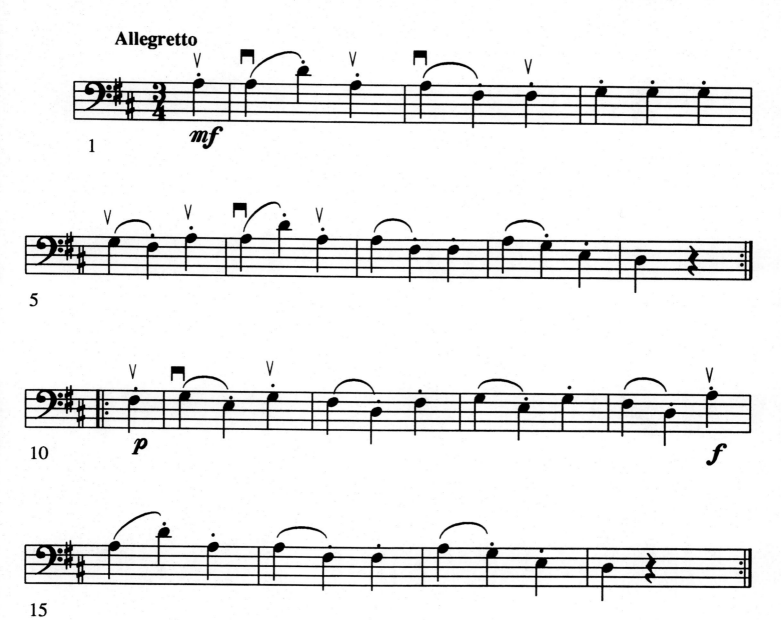

Symphony Theme

Johannes Brahms

Moderato

Dona Nobis Pacem

Latin Hymn

17

Ash Grove

Welsh Melody

PIANO ACCOMPANIMENT

easy
solos for
beginning
cello

level 1

by craig duncan

1 2 3 4 5 6 7 8 9 0

Contents

	Cello	Piano
Russian Dance Tune	4	4
Ode to Joy (Beethoven)	5	5
Kum Bah Yah	6	6
Country Gardens	7	7
Yankee Doodle	8	8
Largo from *The New World Symphony* (Dvorak)	9	9
Fanfare Minuet (Duncombe)	10	10
King William's March (Clarke)	11	11
Dixie (Emmett)	12	12
Gavotte (Telemann)	13	14
Soldier's March (Schumann)	14	15
German Dance (Beethoven)	15	16
Symphony Theme (Brahms)	16	17
Dona Nobis Pacem	17	18
Ash Grove	18	19

Russian Dance Tune

Folk Song

ritard 2nd time

ritard 2nd time

4

Ode to Joy

Ludwig van Beethoven

5

Kum Bah Yah

African Folk Melody

Country Gardens

English Dance Tune

Yankee Doodle

American Folk Tune

Largo
from The New World Symphony

Anton Dvorak

Fanfare Minuet

William Duncomb

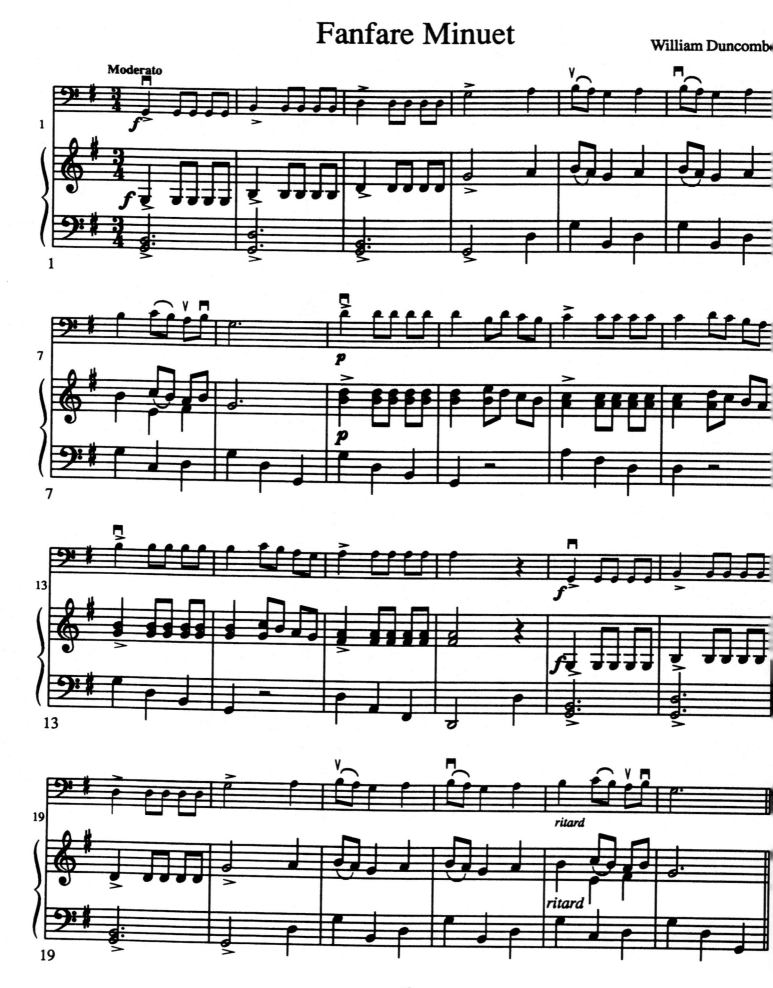

King William's March

Jeremiah Clarke

11

Dixie

D. D. Emmett

Gavotte

Georg Philipp Telemann

Soldier's March

from Album for the Young

Robert Schumann

German Dance

Ludwig van Beethoven

16

Symphony Theme

Johannes Brahms

Dona Nobis Pacem

Latin Hymn

Ash Grove

Welsh Melody